Whispers in the Wind

a collection
of poetry

JEANINE ALLISON

© 2001 by Jeanine Allison. All rights reserved.

No part of this book may be reproduced, stored in a retrieval system, or transmitted by any means, electronic, mechanical, photocopying, recording, or otherwise, without written permission from the author.

ISBN: 0-7596-7136-2

This book is printed on acid free paper.

Cover Design,
Editing and Typesetting
by Bonnie Toews

Graphic for Disc of Life
by Alan S. Bates

1stBooks – rev. 10/26/01

Whispers in the Wind

Wind, water and waves
Whisper as we wend
Our way down the
River of Life.

Silken rays of sunshine
Shimmer on the shiny
Crests, and sparkle
Reflections on azure seas.

Fluffy white clouds
Float across a
Bright blue happy
Sky above.

A purring cat-like
Contentment warms
Our hearts—hoping
For smiles returned.

A celebration of serenity—
And solitude—
A song of praise!

Contents

DEDICATION xi

ACKNOWLEDGEMENTS xiii

INTRODUCTION xv

CANADA 1

    Someday 3
    Bombardment 3
    Futility 4

HOME 5

    Home 7
    Smile 8
    Summer Rains 8
    Dream Port 9
    Summertime in the City 10
    On Becoming Greek 11
    A New Start 12
    Mediterranean Summer 13
    A Solitary Path 14
    In My Own Home 15
    The Pull of the Southern Flame 16
    Migrants 17
    Chain 18
    Springtime in Athens 19
    Gathering Forces 20
    Home for Christmas 21
    Solitude 22
    Butterflies and Flowers 23
    Summer Evening at Paeania 24
    Summer Serenade 25
    A Single Candlestick 26
    Dreams and Choices 27
    New Neighbors 28
    Ode to Athens 29

AWAY 31

    Crossroads 33
    Night Jasmine in Spain 34
    On the Road to Lisbon 35
    Coming Back from Delphi 36
    The Road of Life 37
    Fragrance 38
    Summer Sea at Itea 39
    Easter in Crete 40
    Odyssean Voyage 41
    Maltese Memories 42
    Memories of Majorca 43
    Fire! in Majorca 44
    Illetas Evening 45
    Twilight Time in Portals Nous 46
    Christmas in Sparta 48
    Life is a Journey 48
    Istanbul Interlude 50

DISCO 51

    The Disco 53
    Passion 54
    Multiple Choice 54
    Beginning and Ending 55
    Dancing 56
    Feelings 57
    The Hunt 58
    Ode to Young Men 59
    Eye Games 60
    Another 61
    And Yet Another 61

LOVERS & OTHERS 63

    Relationships 65
    Comfortable 66
    Almost 66
    Yesterday 67
    Empty People 68

The Takers 69
The Rocky Road of Love 70
Trust 70
¡NO! 71
One Night Stand 72
Sex 73
An Old Flame 74
The Root of All Evil 75
In Transit 76
He's A Butterfly! 77
The End 78
Paradoxes and Changes 80

CAT COMPANIONS 81

Head on Paws 83
A Companionable Cat 84
My Cat 85
Summer Siesta 86
Capricorn Cats 87
Night 87
My Matiko 88
Beloved Matiko 89
Renewal 90
Night Watching 91
Unity 92
Seldom 92
In The Shade of the Lilac 93
To Tiko 93
Matiko 94
Ode to Tiko 94
Morning Reverie 94
Two Purrfect Pets 95

SPIRITUAL 97

Blossoms in Spring 101
Time's Healing hands 101
The Occult* 102
The Future 102
A Dream…a Warning 103

vii

The Shadow of Your Wings 103
The Waiting Game 104
Home Safe Harbor 105
Easter Renewal 106
A Little Prayer 107

REFLECTIONS 109

What If? 111
Spanish Poem 112
Misty Memories 113
Promises 114
Peek 114
Ripples on the Pond 115
Dewdrops 116
Time 117
A Tarot Reading 118
Reflections on a Rainy Night 119
Surfing 120
Search for Myself 122
First Day Confusion 123
Phantoms 124
Arachne* 125
At a Crossroads 126
Choices, Dreams and Circles 127
Life Isn't Fair! 128
Paradoxes and Circles of Life 128
My World 129
Webs 130
I Am What I Am! 131
Determination 132
Face It! 133
Free 134
Hidden Mirror 134
Around 135
Under Capricorn 136
In the Candle Glow 137
The Game 138
The World Turns 139
The Surface of Life 140
Ebb Tide 141
Nostalgia 142

Christmas Cards 143
If 144
A Song for Friendship 145
Letters 146
Masquerade 147
Fragments of Joy 148
Rainbow of Life 149
After the Play 150
Solid 151
The Key 151
Cobwebs and Cables 152
I Hear Greece Rejoicing 153

AFTERWORD 155

Thoughts and Questions 157

ABOUT THE AUTHOR 159

Dedication

To all the cats and cat people
in my life—May, Stacie,
Bonnie, my mother,
Mary and
so many others.

Acknowledgements

Bonnie Toews, my editor/designer and
closest friend who pushed me
to collect my poetry;

Allan S. Bates, who graphically
created my "Disc of Life"
and acted as our consultant;

The Rainbow Writing Group
in Athens, Greece,
with whom I have been invited
to write several times;

The music that has inspired me—
of Abba, the Eurythmics and
especially Kris Kristofferson;

Eleni Vainas and
the poetry readings
at Compendium Bookstore,
Athens, Greece, and
Chapters Bookstore,
Newmarket, Canada

Introduction

Open me like a meadow lily.

Inside are many hidden dreams and ideas, values and ideals; it takes time to blossom! Nurturing is necessary. Time to grow. A dormant stage, and then the time is ripe for the bud to open. The sunlight of encouragement smiles down, and the lily stretches outward tender curving petals to reveal the sweetness within, protected until Providence provides the impetus.

* * *

As a trilingual (English, Spanish, Greek—in that order) world traveler, I firmly believe that home is where the heart is or, perhaps more accurately, the heart is where it finds its home. Since my first trip there, I have had, as one fellow-traveler put it, "a love affair with the Mediterranean," so these sentiments often find their way into either the *Home* or *Away* sections of my poetry. Studies and a varied career path, including teaching, counseling, tour guiding, advertising and consulting for Penguin Books, have led me through many countries in Europe, South America, Africa and the Middle East. In addition, I have explored many parts of my native Canada, the United States and the islands of the Caribbean.

In this collection of English poetry spanning thirty years, my divergent interests and poetic voice can be heard—with a beloved cat companion one of my few constants in a changing scene from *Canada* to *Reflections*.

And as our voyage continues, Sweetie (like Tiko before her) and I are still collecting stamps in our passports.

Jeanine Allison, December 2001

JEANINE ALLISON

Canada

JEANINE ALLISON

The following are a group of poems written in 1975, before I left Canada to travel, write more seriously and really search for a new place and way of life.

Someday

In the never-never land
Of far away
Someday I'll find
The place in which
I'll stay,
But 'til I do
I can only say,
"Ah, for peace of mind."

Bombardment

Endless tests and trials
Always on my mind
Searching for something
That I can never find.

Is it in the cards
To ever be at rest?
Searching, searching
Always
Just to meet another test.

Futility

We are always
Searching and
Working towards
Something we can
Never attain
Our work is all
In vain.

We are always
Trying hard
To redeem
Something we
Would not esteem
Even in a dream.

We are always
Dreaming and
Wishing and
Hoping for
Something we
Cannot have
Ever! Ever!

And so
We live in vain.

Home

Home

More and more as Time marches on
I need my sanctuary, hidden

From the workaday world, problems
Stresses of unreasonable expectations.

The drudgery of a day job becomes
Ever more demanding, time-intense,

The quiet desperation turned vocal
The need for quiet retreat ever

More insistent, my music issuing
An invitation to relax, to meditate —

My cat giving her love and her
Companionship as usual, her

Soft purrs, questioning voice, a
Welcome interruption in my reverie —

My books and journals, letters
And poetry, magazines and prayers!

The following is a symbol poem dedicated to my school on our Orientation Day in September 1997. It represents my attitude toward teaching and learning.

Smile

Supportive
Meaningful
Individualized
Learning
Environment

Summer Rains

The summer rains fall gently on the ground;
The soft warm earth welcomes the rhythmic patter;
The land lies wrapped in a protective mist,
And the promises of Persephone seek fruition.

The parched leaves raise their heads gratefully
To gather the drops like dew from Heaven;
The flowers smile and nod, and bloom in joy
As an abiding peace and serenity envelops all.

Dream Port

Reality and unreality
Circles and spirals,
Drifting and dreaming.

The world turns;
The wheel of fortune spins;
My mind goes round.

In and out of the mists,
Back and forth in time,
Over and under the limit.

My ship of dreams sails on
The calm and windless sea
And back in memory.

The haze suddenly clears,
The port looms ahead —
Harbor, haven, home.

Summertime in the City

The neighborhood noise —
Stella's piano mistakes,
The mother and daughter
Screaming at each other
Across the road
But loud, as if
In my own living room,
Beside my typewriter.

A dog barks high on the hill,
And Tiko looks
As bored by it all
As usual;
She's heard it all before.

Another summer evening
With open windows
And lives
Unrelentingly exposed
To each other.

On Becoming Greek

I crossed the Rubicon
Today, no looking back.
A step into unknown
Territory, unsure of a
Foothold, aware of the
Danger of a sudden slip.

I want to retreat into
Myself, hold on to
What is dear to me,
Gather my strength
For whatever lies
Ahead on my unmarked
Path —a little
Apprehensive of how
To handle ensuing
Struggles. How strong
Is friendship? Who
Can really be trusted?
Do I already look at
The world through
Different eyes?

A New Start

A welcoming smile.
Relaxed and informal,
Shown to an office
That's comfortable
And tidy.
Given materials to
Work with,
Necessary details
Explained.
The feeling of trust
And confidence
Returned.
Interesting students
Bright, friendly staff.

It's like coming home!

Mediterranean Summer

The heavy, sweet, summer smell
Of flowers by the roadside,
Reminders of Spain,
Somehow a little sad,
Not just now — in nostalgia —
But always.

The delicious heat on a
Soft evening breeze
Swirls around me,
Comforting,
Drying tears,
Before they're shed.

A Solitary Path

Walking down an old urban street
As dusk descended to soften the cityscape
I gazed into a tiny, ground-floor flat
In a building constructed many years ago,
Obviously well past its heyday.
The French windows were open
To the street, to allow whatever
Stray breezes might waft by to
Enter, to relieve the heat of
A sultry summer evening—
Heavy with the sweet smell
Of Mediterranean fragrant flowers.
In that front room were
Four chairs and only one round
Table, its exact origin masked
By a cheerful white cloth,
And a happy bouquet of red roses
Perched bravely in a mock crystal vase
As the table's centerpiece.
In the right rear corner sat a small
Black and white TV, set on low volume;
And in the right front corner
The simple cotton frock covering the knees
Of the room's single occupant could be seen.
The rest of her ageless, impersonal
Body and face masked by the
White lacy curtains pulled back
From the windows and stirred by the
Welcome breeze. I could imagine
A little narrow hall outside of the
Single door at the back of the room
Leading to an equally tiny sparsely
Furnished bedroom, neat and

Well-dusted, with a simple
Old-fashioned wardrobe at one end.
Beside it would be a small
Bathroom with its ancient tub,
Toilet, bidet and basin, sparkling
Clean like the compact kitchen
Next door. Its contents would
Include a half-fridge, a two-burner
Cooker with a small oven,
An old-style marble sink and
A few cupboards to store her
Dishes, pots and pans.
The home of a lady
In her twilight years, solitary
Only or also lonely, I wondered, as
I wound my own solitary path
Down the street towards home.

In My Own Home

The home of the heart —
Holding fast to dreams and
Memories, of having friends
To share the happiness
Of heavenly health-renewing
Rest, relaxation, restoring
The energy and determination
To face the future,
To overcome the obstacles
Life strews along the path
To ultimate fulfillment.

The Pull of the Southern Flame

I came to live in southern climes
With warmth of the sun, memorable times,
Freedom to fight for what I want
Deaf to every unreasonable taunt.

Sunshine bathes me in healing light;
Moonlight joyfully illumines the night;
Candles of the sky — the twinkling stars —
Make me oblivious e'en to honking cars.

People filled with passion care —
I can feel it in the air;
Where I belong, where I must stay
To live, to fight, to share their way.

Migrants

You ask how it is. I will tell you.
Women writing.
A writing community.
Sharing experiences.
We are the survivors!
Long-time residents
In a once-foreign land.
Adapted to the sounds
And rhythms of another
Language
Culture
Mentality.
Now the rhythms form
A background beat
To the daily round
Of trivia and temptations
Torn from the workaday
World, rescued for
Reflections in
Languid leisure.
Settled into a
More comfortable
Middle-age
Haven—Home.
This was not to be expected!

Chain

Links …
Events …
Ideas …
Daisy chains …
The tie that binds.

Broken links,
Seemingly unconnected
Events,
Ideas linked
and interlinked,
A daisy chain
of summer memories
Nostalgic impressions
of summer days
Childhood joys
on grandfather's farm.

The bonds of family
Shared circumstances
The chain of life.

Springtime in Athens

A gentle sun caresses the skin
Nature's springtime kiss—
It will become too ardent
In the summer, in the scorching heat
That burns and repels
Like the ardour of an overanxious suitor.

But now in the awareness
Of the life sprung anew
Jade green leaves flutter overhead
A proud silken perfection of nature's art.

Cats bask in the warmth
And smile their gratitude
To the sky, stretching lazy paws
And turning up a vulnerable tummy
In a time-honored gesture of trust and hope.

Gathering Forces

How we all need the time
To be removed from the
Daily grind, the rat race
(And we're all the rats!)
The stultifying routine
The unrelenting pressure
Of schedules to follow
Deadlines to meet,
Projects to complete,
No time to *be*!

Creative juices cannot flow
When all our energy
Is directed at simply
Surviving and keeping up!

How we all need to step back
To be observers
Not always thrusting
Participants and leaders
In the career game.

Rest and relaxation,
Planned withdrawal,
In comfortable surroundings —
To meditate and gather strength
To enter the fray
To take our "rightful places"
Come fall classes.

Home for Christmas

The Christmas holidays
Have started today,
Time for the cat
To cuddle and play.

A warm and cozy
Comfortable retreat,
Warm conversation
And plenty to eat.

The joy of the season
Comes into our hearts;
We hope that it
Will never depart.

The cheerful tree
With balls and lights,
Blocks out the
Daily strife and fights.

No need to travel
To unfamiliar climes,
It's at home where we
Have our best times!

Solitude

My kitty curled on my lap,
A soft paw keeping light
From her eyes.

Shutters closed, locking out
A still chilly night
In late April.

Relaxation, renewal, withdrawal
From the workaday world
Of stress and care.

Much needed time to reflect,
To regain the fortitude
To meet the challenges.

Time to be immersed in
Private thoughts, reading,
Music, selected TV —

A tribute to Queen bringing
Memories of unforgettable
Concerts in Spain.

Roberto Carlos on Spanish TV —
Death, ageing, disease,
Real-life threats.

Home – a refuge, rest,
Sleep, dreams, Easter:
Joy and old friends.

Praise, worship, fellowship,
Sharing, caring — another
Easter has come and gone!

Butterflies and Flowers

A butterfly flutters
Soft powdery fragile
Wings, fanning gently,
Slow insistent progress
In a pastel yellow blur

Deep pink, blossoms
Smile open: faces raised
To the welcoming sun
Of Athens, February spring—
A promise amidst problems!

Summer Evening at Paeania

The audience, sitting on hastily arranged
White plastic chairs, in the courtyard
Of the Vorres Museum*,
Some elegantly attired, others
Casually dressed.

The performer, the beautiful Liona Boyd
Enchanting all of us
With her concert on
Classical guitar.

Nature's chorus also joining in,
But their accompaniment
More appreciated by the audience
Than the artist!

First, the cicadas forming an orchestra
In the soft summer night,
Their insistent strumming
Keeping rhythmic time
Though themselves hidden from view.
They drew our eyes to the
Romantically lit tree trunks
Standing proud and tall
Behind the roof of the Art
Gallery, which now became the
Backdrop for the
Soloist sitting just in front.

* Vorres Museum at Paeania outside of Athens, Greece.

During the second half
The cicadas lulled
Themselves to sleep;
Then, as Liona played
Spanish-influenced pieces,
Another musician
Added his voice.
This time, a tiny owl
Perched on a tree branch,
Hooted along in joy,
Reflecting his appreciation.
He and his harmony
Brought smiles
To the lips of many
Seated in the audience.

Nature's creatures reminded us
That this was their home,
And we were only guests.

Summer Serenade

The cicadas strum their summer serenade
And Athens drowses in lazy lassitude
In mid-August pause to refresh,
Recharge those lagging batteries, ready
For the inevitable challenge *Winter*
Beginnings soon bring, to stir
Us all into action once again!

Musing on memories of simpler times,
Gentler attitudes, less hurried approaches
To a life still lived to the limit,
And the wine of happiness and sorrow
Drunk to the lees.

A Single Candlestick

On the old-fashioned round wooden
Dining room table, covered with a
Spanish lace tablecloth, sat a
Single silver candlestick holding
A plain white candle, flickering
In the deepening twilight
The table was set for one,
But with attractive quilted placemat
And matching napkin, old but
Well-shined silver cultlery
Waiting for the cherished
China plates and dishes
To make the setting complete.
An antique china cup and saucer,
A reminder of years gone by,
Sat on the left; a crystal
Wineglass and matching waterglass
Were waiting to be filled.
The guest-and-hostess-in-one
Entered the cozy room, carrying
The attractively arranged dinner
On a silver tray, which also held
Small bottles of Portuguese Vinho Verde
And Perrier water, sparkling.
The meal served, she was seated
Her only companion — but all that
Was necessary — was her beloved
White Persian cat, green eyes
Closing in the candle's glow,
Purring with satisfaction and contentment.
Solitary elegance and aloofness
Embodied in both pet and mistress.

Dreams and Choices

The cicadas sing softly
In the pine trees
In the park, on a lazy
Sultry summer August night.
Athens is deserted as
Residents have fled to
Sunsets on islands or
Distant shores, homesick for
Their *real* home, while they
Rest and replenish, looking
At their reflections in still glass
Lakes, mirrored in shop windows
Or in hotels' glittering glass panes.

Music playing in the background
Setting the pace and place
Thankful for the respite
From toil and trouble
Of the workaday world we all
Re-enter much too soon.

New Neighbors

Some new neighbors moved in today
New faces and friends across the way.

Sharing summer evenings, languid and long
As easy to relate to as a favorite song.

Things to arrange, old possessions in new places
Trying to fit in like old familiar faces.

A neighborhood, we live with each other's quirks
A bit of tolerance, and somehow it all works!

Sweetie sits on the balcony in her adopted chair,
Watching the proceedings, taking the night air.

An old-fashioned place, we relate to each other,
The curiosity, the caring, the hint of a mother.

Ode to Athens
(on a summer night)

We live in the center
Of a great city,
Pulsing with the
Lifeblood of a
Vital people.

The noisy sounds
Of insistent traffic,
Dogs barking,
Joyful exclamations,
Muffled curses,
Shouted expressions
Of dismay,
And anger
And determination.

Life lived
With an intensity
From heartfelt ecstasy
To the deepest sorrow
Always striving
To defeat adversity,
Not merely survive!

Away

Crossroads

There are many crossroads
   in our lives and
      baffling forks in the road.

Often we wonder which
   way to turn, which
      choice will prove correct.

And even many years thereafter
   we ponder our decision
      evaluating it again.

Of course it's a forced choice
   and we can never
      really turn back.

How difficult all would have
   been, we tell ourselves
      if only...

And once again I face
   not just one of these
      but a superhighway traffic circle

With overpasses and bridges
   of different levels and
      roads in a labyrinth of

Directions, not straight, but
   in circles and spirals
      and right-angled turns.

At the same time, in midlife
   It's time for a change—
      I'm ready to take the risk.

Life is a game of chance
   with prizes and many
      disappointments along the way,

But meant to be played
   boldly, with determination
      and the will to win.

And so I'll choose another road
   right or wrong, difficult
      or easy, but mine.

Night Jasmine in Spain

Jasmine wafting on the evening air—
A feeling of peace surges
Through my veins,
A renewal of body and soul.
A smile touches my lips
Like a promise of gentleness.
The Future holds out
Her hand and adventure
Beckons subtly in a
Conspiracy of secret
Pleasures to be tasted,
Savored and enjoyed;
Then stored in memory
'Till nostalgia knocks
And wakens…
Remembrance like old
Yellowed lace.

On the Road to Lisbon

Security. No, I
    never really
        wanted that,

A life stretching
    ahead of me like
        a smooth freeway —

No unexpected curves
    Or bumps or
        unmarked turns.

The unexplained or
    unexplainable
        mystery, excitement,

This was instead
    the avenue I chose
        and choose.

For these I traded
    comfort, routine
        a well-worn path,

To chart an unfamiliar
    course in foreign
        lands and feelings.

To seek the challenge
    of whatever may
        lie around the bend.

The rewards are those
    that come to the
        adventurers, fighters,

Who set out on a
    journey, not knowing
        the ultimate destination.

It's difficult, yes,
    but never boring,
        no time for regrets.

Coming Back from Delphi

The late afternoon sun slants
    across the fields
Deepening the green of the trees
    and yellow of flowers;
The serenity of fulfillment,
    of meeting old friends
Encloses my heart as
    Zephyr rustles the leaves
And the beauty of the view
    gladdens my soul.
The wheat nods in the breeze
    as the road winds slowly
Ahead of us; heading home,
    happy to be here.
Sun and shadow on the
    mountains…

The Road of Life

Just a wanderer
Down Life's highway
Awaiting the next
Way station enroute.

A stop-rest and
Perhaps relaxation,
Or maybe more
Problems to fill
Our time.

We drive uncertainly
Into the night;
Anonymous headlights
Confronting us,
No comfort
In a shared journey
With those heading
In the same direction,
Either.
We have our own
Paths to follow,
Our own turns
To make,
Different detours,
Various paces.

Fragrance

The spice of life,
Heavy, sweet jasmine,
Nostalgia for many
Mediterranean summers
Here, and in Spain—
My love affair with
The Mediterranean has
Perfumed my life…
The fragrance of flowers,
The aroma of basil,
Oregano, flavorful garlic
Inviting me to taste a
Greek or Spanish dish;
Intense lemony-sweet
Spanish male cologne
Wafting across the
Seaside air in Cariheula*,
And in the background
The tempting odor of
Fresh-caught fish sizzling
In virgin olive oil…
All these scents and more
Fill me with their
Fragrance of freedom.

*Cariheula is a little fishing village near Torremolinos, Spain.

Summer Sea
(at Itea)*

The waves softly lap the shore —
A peaceful, restful to and fro
Like a cat licking silky fur;

The sun smiles; the palm trees
Whisper as the cicadas sing
Their song of joy.

And in the background
The mountains stand guard
Wrapped in their hazy blue mist,
And an almost cloudless
Azure sky spreads like a
Protective umbrella overhead.

Little fishing boats at rest
In the harbor, sailboats unfurl
Their sails and sleep,
While sunlight dances and
Sparkles on cresting waves.
Itea — in the lazy August
Smugness of perfect contentment.

* Itea is a seaside village near Delphi, Greece.

Easter in Crete

Myriads of white daisies
Like snow on the hillsides;
The shock of bright red poppies
Interspersed with small yellow
Wildflowers — wild and free —
Symbolic of the wild and free
Spirit of Crete,
In time present and time past.

Insistent church bells
Toll in the afternoon
Hammering home the messages
Of the Holy Week.
Reminders of suffering
And death abound
But hope springs anew
And victory is proclaimed
In Christ's Resurrection.

Odyssean Voyage
(On the ferry from Kefalonia to Ithaca)

Kindling flames of desire —
Earnestly searching
For the road to
All that is enticing.
Lost among the rubble of
Ordinary life,
Needing something to stimulate
Inertia into
Action.

All of us on a
Never ending journey,
Destined to discover

Inside of each of us
The hope so long
Hidden from view,
All of us travelers,
Curious to reach our own
All-important Ithaca – home.

Maltese Memories

The empty winds are creaking
Who tell us tales of astonishing stones!
Memorials to a distant past—
Perhaps before the time
Of the Crusades.

An eerie place, a sense of having
Been there before, of touching
The light-beige weathered rocks
Before time had smoothed out
All the jutting edges.

A sanctuary full of meaning
But now inaccessible, just beyond
The threshold of conscious memory.
A powerful impression of
Significant events.

An overwhelming sensation
Of having been a part of
Rituals and ceremonies
Once as familiar as my name,
Locked now in eternity.

Another lifetime, being a young
Woman, feeling the feathery fingers
Of a whispering wind, carrying, the
Message from Malta, across time:
"But I was young and foolish and
now am full of tears"

Memories of Majorca

A trip back in time, emotions
Feelings, remembered friends,
The way it used to be.
A glimpse of the clock
Turned back twenty years
To a way of life that no longer
Exists—a simpler time
I tell myself, but was it really?

The best and the worst times
Of life I've spent on Spanish soil
And if this trip I didn't
Experience the supreme highs
I didn't touch the deepest
Depths, either—a smoother path
Worn by Life's lessons
And acceptance taught in
Life's lengthening shadows.

New friends, refreshments and
Renewal through new lessons
To be learned. People gathered
From all corners of the globe,
Drawn by wanting to be better,
To return to our native
Or adopted countries with more
To share with colleagues and
Our students, from within ourselves.

Fire!
(in Majorca)

The sun is blood-red
As seen through the branches
Of the pine trees.
It signifies the danger
The pain of a beautiful
Forest burning —
Great gulping tongues of
  Fire
Devour the life-sustaining
  Trees
Endanger the surrounding
  Homes
Of wildlife and humans
  Alike.

Billowing clouds of odious
Grey smoke
Choke the air
And Suffocating fumes
Drift over the
Suffering land
  For miles.

Fire-fighting water-filled
Planes criss-cross
Overhead,
Discharge their precious
Cargo to choke
The dreaded enemy
Of island-summer
Where tinder — dry
Leaves and branches
Are always vulnerable
To the destructive monster —
  Fire!

Illetas Evening
(Illetas, near Palma, Majorca)

The full moon traces
A silvery path
On the tranquil sea.
The road to dreams —
An invitation
To open your heart
And your arms
To all within
The realm of possibility
However remote.

A plane drones overhead
And the first star
Twinkles to life.
Palm trees immobile,
Like ghostly guards
On the promontory
Beside a turquoise
Lighted pool and
Umbrellas folded
Like praying hands
Across the little
Protected bay.

A few cars crawl
Along the road
And the sound of
Contented conversation
Of diners drifts
Across the early
Evening air
From one side
Balanced by
A soft melodious
Spanish singer
From the other —
An Illetas evening.

Twilight Time in Portals Nous

Night falls softly on the hills
In the background,
And out in the placid bay.
Across the water
Green, blue, red, and white
Lights start to twinkle
Like the odd barely visible
Star in a gray-blue clear sky.
The half-moon glows
Increasingly brighter.
The sky at the horizon
Is tinged with pinkish orange
And a lighthouse flashes
Its slow steady warning
At the end of a
Finger of land
Jutting into the sea
At the entrance to
The harbor.
Streetlights start to light up
Quiet residential streets
Almost devoid of cars
Or pedestrians.
The turquoise-blue of the
Pool below issues
A welcoming invitation
To taste its delicious
Soothing warmth and refreshments.

The coniferous trees,
Palm trees and cacti
Stand like silent sentinels
In the gardens
And along the streets.
Softly a little breeze
With restful evening coolness
Starts to stir across
The land.
Lights sparkle from ships
Moored in the bay.
A few dogs are barking
In different yards
Far away, and
The drone of a plane engine
Sounds from out
A little way over the water.
The horizon – sky then
Flushes pinkish purple;
The moon really shines;
More lights flash on
In apartment buildings
And villas on
Every side.
The peace and joy
Settles over the land
Like a bedtime prayer.

Christmas in Sparta

With the sheltering hills
Snow-topped, majestic
The music of Christmas
And singers and children —
The warmth, the joy,
The sharing, the caring —
For this I chose
This country, these people
To be my own — and I
To be one of them!

Life is a Journey

On the road to Ithaca
How well I recall
The greens ever-changing,
The soft olive green with
Silvery tones underneath,
The velvety deep green
Of the cedars and pines
On the hills.
The little clustered bushes
On the faraway hills
And beside the road.

The open road, twists and turns.

JEANINE ALLISON

A straight road, as in
Canada, could never
Satisfy the heart that
Yearns for and feels
The challenge of the
Winding road — "never to
Know what lies around
The next bend,"
Be it danger, a triumph,
A challenge. I anticipate
Whatever comes with —
If not equanimity then
Something close, and
An acceptance of life
I could never have
Gained in my "native land."

And on that journey
A couple of months ago
To Kefalonia and Ithaca,
I stopped in Kefalonia,
But as a friend observed
I didn't have to travel on
Because I've found
My 'Ithaca'* ¡*Verdad!***

* *Ithaca,* a poem by Constantine Cavafy, Greek poet.
** ¡Verdad – true

Istanbul Interlude

Sitting by the silky azure sea,
The sun's rays spreading
A silvery carpet over
Gently rising swells,
Ships drifting lazily by —
An invitation to walk along
The sandy crescent-shaped
Shore, thoughts meandering
Back to other visits,
Misplaced friends, displaced
Lives, shared good times.

Life like the sea moves on,
Carrying with it, bits and
Pieces, some significant
Others not, attachments,
Ideas, emotions, connections,
Made and broken,

Seagulls happily splash
In the turquoise pool —
Their giant birdbath —
Contentment!

Disco

JEANINE ALLISON

The Disco
(A Poem in Prose)

The music surrounds me, the pulsating rhythm a protective cocoon, shutting out the usually inconsistent everyday problems. The soft red lights spread like a fluffy cloud and let me float out of reach of mortals into a dream world that is surreal — my only reality and a *fantasma**.

Beware all those who enter here — it's addicting! Some come to remember, some to forget, the good times and the bad times, each necessary for the other. Some come to meet old friends, others to avoid enemies, real and imaginary, people and *pensamientos***.

But in this labyrinth of time and space, it's too easy to be caught in the trap that is both binding and the door to freedom — the only freedom, which is a state of mind.

* Fantasma — ghost
** Pensamientos — thoughts

Passion

Perfect
Articulation…
Sizzling
Scenes…
Intent
On
Night passion!

Multiple Choice

And so
What would you like
Me to say?
You promised to come
And you didn't.
- a) I'm disappointed.
- b) I'm pissed off.
- c) I believed you.
- d) You're just a man (after all!).
- e) It doesn't matter.
- f) All of the above.
- g) None of the above.

Anyway —
It's your choice;
You made it
That way!

Beginning and Ending

The vultures. Yes,
They're here tonight.
All of them —
Old and young,
Waiting and watching —
Just for
One chance.

A chance? Yes,
A chance to be
A real part
Of the world
That passes them by.

They are observers
When it's not
A spectator sport —
Living.

Living and feeling,
Pain and sorrow,
Happiness and joy.

The world's a stage
But they're here
In the audience
Unwitting listeners
To others' conversations.

But I'm also part
Of the play, or
Am I?

Dancing

I step tentatively into your arms—
The music's dreamy,
An invitation,
Dare we step closer?

Each does, a little—
My hand moves on your shoulder;
Like a caress
Yours goes up my back.

Our cheeks find a resting place,
And we relax
Into each other's
Body contours.

We sway to the music
Relaxed now,
Getting closer,
Our feet, too, in harmony.

And then I feel
Your urgency, your
Wanting, your hardness,
And we press closer.

The music ends,
And we step back a little,
Our arms around
Each other—communicating.

"What is dancing but
making love set to music?"
Ah yes, and if
We dance like this,
It's inevitable.

Feelings

They say that I don't really care,
My reactions hang in the air.

But they live on the surface of life —
They only talk about the strife.

I give not just an easy smile,
No outstretched hand, without a trial.

No kisses without the feeling —
The passions that send the senses reeling.

The warmth, the closeness, the fire,
The contest of which I never tire.

"The contest! Is it then a game?"
They ask. But isn't theirs the same?

At least my players are real;
They do and say what they really feel.

It's no casual peck on the cheek,
Forgotten quickly — in less than a week.

The feeling, the memories stay,
I'll have them yet another day.

The sharing, the giving, with truly
No thought of tomorrow, a life unruly.

No neat packages of parts,
Locked away in sections of hearts.

Exactly what I say, I think,
And though I'm often on the brink —

And perhaps one day I'll fall,
And someone will catch me, or that's all —

But I will never step back in fear,
Their timid warnings I cannot hear.

The Hunt

In the world
where
I am both the hunter
and
the hunted,
I rejoice
in the thrill
of the chase.

Sometimes
it's good
to be caught
or to capture
the prize
myself.

Sometimes
it's better
to elude
my pursuers
"to live
to fight
another day."

Captivity,
however,
is momentary,
and like all
fleeting pleasures
therefore, to be
savored.

It adds
spice to life;
not for me
bland acceptance.

It is the struggle
that keeps me
alive
and relishing
each new
taunt.

A touch of danger
like icing
on a cake,
sometimes
reached for
with a quick
yet hesitant
finger.

Impossible
to repeat—
in repetition
is death
of feelings.

Ode to Young Men

Sturdy and strong,
Sexy and virile;
Why say it's wrong?
Give them a trial!
Joyful and willing,
Attentive and caring;
I *know* it's thrilling,
If a bit 'wearing'!

Excitement and love,
Affection and kisses,
They sure can prove
How an older one misses!

Eye Games

We play eye games
In the mirror
Over the bar.
I watch the
Reflections
And so do you
And suddenly
Our eyes meet
And hold, and
Then I drop mine.
I stare in my drink;
I look somewhere
Else.
And your eyes
Follow me
Questioning,
"Is she interested?
How do I get her
To notice me?
If I talk to her,
How will she
Respond?"

Not sure.

Back to eye games.

Another

Another loser
  just walked in;

I think I'll have
  another gin.

No, I can't be bothered
  to try

To talk to another
  boring guy.

Another night at
  the neighborhood bar.

Another encounter
  that won't go far.

Untitled

And tonight's
golden prick awards
    go to
the cowboys and the Greeks
on the dance floor.

The queers' convention
and the conventional queers
    the hookers
    the gigolos
    the wierdos
      the regulars
and the regular wierdos
      the professional studs
      the barrels with feet
the Japanese tourist trap
the American businessmen
    (dull as usual)
      the Frenchmen
and the doll in drag.

Another night
at the Galaxy Bar.

JEANINE ALLISON

*Lovers
&
Others*

Relationships

Friends, lovers, acquaintances,
Students, neighbors, colleagues,
Bosses, business associates,
Fellow teachers, relatives—
How do they all fit in?

Contacts by phone,
By mail,
In person,
In bed.

Suddenly returning
After a long absence
The tie remains intact—
Accepting, slipping into
The old comfortable
Groove again.

But for how long?
I can't count on them
And for this
I remain, a little aloof,
A person apart;
Enjoy... and wave goodbye.

Comfortable

It's comfortable —
to sit in bed on a rainy day
to feel my cat curled on my toes
to sense your love across the miles
to anticipate seeing you again.
and then…
to cuddle close and hold your hand
to share the music that we love
to talk for hours over drinks
to find new places to explore.

Almost

My ex-husband thought
it was beautiful
—*almost*—
probably better
than getting there.

At least we tried.
"This time we almost
made our poem rhyme."

But it doesn't have
To rhyme, you see,
And *almost* isn't
Enough for me.

Yesterday

Yesterday
    when I saw you
    standing there
    proud, erect—
I couldn't help
    running and reaching out
    to touch you,
    to see if
    you were real.
You were—too real, perhaps!

As we sat and talked
    over a coffee
    and you reached out
    to kiss me,
    you wondered why
    I started back.

Oh, we made love
    and it was pleasant
    but it was for
    yesterday.

And when you pulled out
    Two pictures
    Of us together
    Smiling in the warmth
    Of our new love
    Seven years ago—
You, a boy with black hair
    Soft as a cat's,
Me with brilliant red
    And I understood…

    Yesterday.

Empty People

Reaching for something
for nothing,
not knowing that then
it's worth nothing.
The gold will turn to
ashes in their hands
and fly away in the wind.
The bitter desert wind
blows scorching hot
and bitterly cold
and brings with it
no cooling, no relief.

They are the cheaters
but most of all
they cheat themselves.
They play a role
in a drama
always in rehearsal
never performed;
no audience
listens to the anguished
cries that are
ineffectual —
a mockery of life
and real acting.
Every contact is
a means of getting
something —
a free drink,
someone else
to pay for something —
borrowed enjoyment.

They steal or
manipulate
everybody,
everything,
not realizing
that when they
steal their best
friend's girl,
in the process
they lose what
attracted them
in the first place
—the warmth,
the caring, the
sharing—most
of all, they're
incapable of that!
They're empty.
They have nothing
to give.

The Takers

They want *everything*
that they don't have
and they see
others with,
but they're not
willing to pay the
price.
They want the producers,
like me, to pay.

The Rocky Road of Love

Why is it
That someone is always
Available
When for some
Reason or other
It's inconvenient
Or he's not
Wanted
At least, not then?

Maybe we thrive
(or love does)
On the challenge
Of obstacles
To be overcome
Of time, of space,
Of competition,
Of opposition.

When it's too easy…
I guess
We don't bother.

Trust

My mistake
Once again.
He wasn't
Worth it!
When will
I learn?
Not to give
Too much
Of me,
And especially —
Trust!

¡NO!

They want—
my help.
my giving,
my caring,
my affection,
my energy,
my laughter.

But what is
my part of
this bargain?

An empty
"Thank you,"
a meaningless
smile,
a gift
I don't like.

And then…

Their scorn
for being
tolerant enough,
weak enough—
too bright
too feeling—

¡N0!

One Night Stand

He was sitting at the end of the bar
With a J&B and the keys to his car.

He watched me as I came in and sat down
Ready with a line about life in this town.

I didn't look his way but awaited his move,
Wondering what he thought he had to prove.

The accent told me he was Lebanese,
The twinkling eyes, a desire to please.

What approach would he finally make?
And how much time did he think it would take?

The inevitable came, "Your place or mine?"
Somehow surprising, yet a common line.

"I'm thinking about it," I finally said.
He just smiled and nodded his head.

"I'm a good dancer," not a boast but true,
And actually he could be compared with a few.

Intelligent, well-dressed, witty and kind,
A good deal better than I hoped to find.

Not as young as I'd like, but then
In this world, there are *no* perfect men!

A gentle touch, easy confidence, slow smile,
We'd already gone more than the first mile.

Another shot of bourbon, music shared,
The small touches—it seemed he cared.

Libra balance, coolness, a steady stand,
It all worked out just like he planned.

Champagne on ice, a velvet robe,
Soft music, candlelight, a tasty 'lobe.

Playful, sensual, exciting, no need to rush,
Exploring, feeling…a sudden hush.

He took me to the heights of passion,
Making love in his own unique fashion.

Enjoyment, contentment, curled up in his arms,
No need to worry about false alarms.

Sex

Sex is a form of power
A means of control
A game of poker
Straight—or wild cards.

An Old Flame

When the end came
Suddenly but somehow
    Expected
The flood gates of tears
Were released
And for four hours I cried
As if my heart would
    Break
And, you see, it did!

But how does one live
With a broken heart?
    Carefully —
So no one will know,
Not even the owner,
    Sometimes;
But something inside
Me closed
    Permanently.

The Root of All Evil

The lies, the manipulations
You become like the people
You live with. So I love
You, but I don't like
You anymore.

You belong to the world
Of the rich, where money
Talks and rules, and
Turns the world, and
Solves problems, and
Bribes…

Well, I'm not for sale!
I don't have a price.
"I only own myself,
But *all* of me is mine."

I belong to the world
That works,
That tells the truth
Even when
It hurts.

I don't believe in
Getting something
For nothing —
That's not a game
I *ever* play.

Someone to tell
Convenient lies —
So that another
Can take
From the producers.
Well, I'm a producer.
It doesn't fly!

In Transit

Lovers—this is
A way-station in time—
Cozy, warm, welcoming,
But always temporary.
You are transitory,
Only I remain.

Fourteen in four months!
Three nationalities.
A twenty-year span,
Different outlooks,
Various occupations.

I have very cosmopolitan
Tastes in men.
Variety *is* the
Spice of life,
And not for me
Bland, impassionate sex.

Thrill me, pet me,
Sometimes stay the night
And hold me,
Cuddle me. Dance with me
Share the music
Ideas, drinks, company.

Then ¡*Adiós amigo!*

He's A Butterfly!

He flits, stopping only
To taste the nectar
Of the flowers
In his path—
A gentle visitor.

He won't stay,
But then no one
Expects him to—
Appreciator of beauty—
He drinks it in
And departs.

But one day
He'll spread his wings
And fly this way
Again.

Welcome friend!

The End
(Τέλος)

C'est fini.
It's over.
   Τελείωσα.
Adiós, por la última vez.
Arivederci, me piacerebbe.

No matter how
We say it,
Another affair
Has run its course,
And the wrench
Of another parting
Soul felt

And you, my love,
It's not really
Your fault.

Is it mine?
Well, maybe.

Or is it
"Irreconcilable
differences?"

Did it have
To end, this
Way?

Were the seeds
Of its destruction
Sown at the
Beginning of our
Love story?

And you stood
In front of my door
Mutely pleading
With me to say

JEANINE ALLISON

The words that
Could make you
Cross the room
With your
So familiar
Dashing stride,
To crush the doubts
That frequently
Intruded into
Our world
In an ever-loving
Embrace.

Yes, I love you
And I know
That you
Love me.

But I can
No longer
Close my eyes
To the reality
That we cannot
Stay together
For a long time.

It hurts.

My heart cries
But my eyes
Are dry.

You think it's easier
For me because
I've loved and
Known the heartbreak
Of parting, before.

It's not.

You say you hope
You'll never love again.

You will...and be glad.

Paradoxes and Changes

You came so swiftly and stayed
With me.
What happiness with you
By my side in the morning
When I woke!
I became alive for the first time
...in some ways,
but other parts of me had to die.
Knowing all your needs
And giving all I had to give
...for awhile.
I'm yours in this world or
Any other world
...of memories and dreams...
My strong man
Tender man
My man.
But not only mine
As I'm not only yours...
Keep reaching for me,
I'll always be there!
...Maybe.
As long as you remember me,
It will go on and on —
*¡Vivan las veces y las cosas buenas!**

* Long live the good times and the good things of life.

Cat Companions

Head on Paws

You told me not
To put my head down
And give up.

You mistake me,
Sir! The lioness will
Lick her paws,

Rest, curl up,
Sleep — head on paws
Watching warily,

Gather strength
To fight another day —
And win!

This cat's not
Really asleep, but
She knows how

To lull her enemies
Into a sense of
False security.

A Companionable Cat

She crouches low
and with eyes of
black fire
stalks across the
carpet
in the time-honored
tradition of
her feline ancestors.

She crawls under
the covers
and curls on
my toes,
one paw wrapped
possessively
across my ankle.

She sits beside
me when I read,
patiently waiting
to hear her
name.

She perches on
the back of the
love seat and
gazes out the
window at the
birds flying in
growing flocks,
and homeless
cats below.

She becomes
an ornament
on the back
of the armchair,
in the bathroom
sink, and beside
the bedroom lamp.

She curls
contendedly
rolling over and
over in the sun.
Cuddly and charming!

My Cat

She feels my every mood and care,
She makes my troubles float on air;
She cuddles close and purrs and "smiles"
A master of manipulative wiles.
She's company, joy, affection, trial,
A paradox that makes my life worthwhile.

Summer Siesta

The cicadas begin
Their chirping hum
That marks
The sweetness
Of the lazy, late
Summer afternoon.

"Siesta time!"
They call
And I drift
Toward the
Welcoming bed
In drowsy contentment.

Tiko comes too,
Her tail held high
Rubbing against
The doorways,
Purring in
Happy anticipation.

Sleep, dreams, satisfaction!

Capricorn Cats

Life lived to the fullest!
No surface skims for us
Capricorns—to enjoy greatly
To feel deeply, but then
To go on seeking the life-giving
Stimulation. We are the survivors
In an often hostile, challenging
World—adaptable, but always
Solid, dependable and
Constant when it counts.

Night

The night is a black cat
Velvet paws that reach out
And touch you—a gentle reminder
"I'm here close beside you,"
Hiding in the shadows
Watching with
Glowing green eyes
Wary, knowing, secretive, furtive
The magic of hidden powers
Evil, the occult, the unknown.
Danger lurks in sheathed claws
That can tear—
In a paw that caresses.

My Matiko

A life line of hope,
Packaged happiness
In a soft bundle
Of fur and purrs
That hides a will
Of iron, a determination
To do what she wants
Regardless of the
Personal price—
She'll pay.

She is my alter ego
More me than myself
A symbol of a life
Deceptively simple
Seemingly easy.
Wide eyes
Open with an appeal
Of which she's aware—
But like me
Uses only when
It pleases her.
Sometimes she's
Surprised by it, herself.

The tail curls around
The front paws
A neat package...
Watchful, smiling
Aloof, self-contained
The ultimate cat.

Beloved Matiko

My cat comes toward me
Her tail
A question mark.

Lazy stretches, side-to-side
—her happy rolls!
Blinking ecstasy.

She curls her toes
And meows
Adoringly up at me.

Her hazel-gray eyes
Two saucers
Of trust.

"Where have you been?"
"What are you doing?"
"Where's my food?"

A welcoming joy-purr
Making a house
A cozy haven.

Renewal

Almost three weeks' withdrawal,
The ultimate rest 'n relaxation,
Ready to face the world again.

Time to ponder, read 'n write,
Time to explore the inner self
Get those creative juices flowing again.

The ultimate calm is a sitting cat;
Phrases drift in 'n out of consciousness
And I just observe and enjoy.

'Life is a series of little accomplishments' —
Don't expect too much (Cats don't!)
And you will never be disappointed!

I've touched the highs, I've searched the lows
The goin' up is still worth the comin' down —
O yes, Kris, now I know it really is!

And so, catlike as always, I stretch
Forward confident paws, arch my back
And with question-like tail aloft

I saunter forth, with ever-watchful
Green, curious-eyes, to be a part
Of the night-prowl-hunt called life.

Nightwatching

How nice it is to slink the streets at night
To hide in velvety darkness—
Watching and waiting
From twilight to midnight
To see the weird and wonderful
Observed from the wayside.
A welter of whispers,
Wondering wildness
Woeful or wistful.
Winter rains
Spring blossoms
Summer scorching
Autumn crispness—
All pass silently, swiftly
On soft cat paws

But beware "there are claws
That can tear
In a paw that caresses!"

Unity

An outstretched paw on a pillow,
    An arm extending to the edge of the bed,
A soft cat-cheek on my shoulder,
    A nose buried into her mane
An arched back curved against my ribs;
The reflection of shared warmth
    Cuddled and contented —
Our souls are one.

Seldom

Seldom do tears
Fill my eyes
But somehow
I find
That they come
Too easily
When you are
On my mind.

It helps to ease
The pain
Of all the fun
We had
For when I think
Of "us"
I always feel
Sad.

In The Shade of the Lilac

Whisper sleeps eternally
Beneath the mauve lilac tree.
A warm memory, a joy
To remember with a toy.
How she loved to jump and play!
A friend and companion every day.
God's love embodied on earth
I'm still grateful for her birth.

Sleep on my dear departed cat,
The affection, happiness pets that
I gave, and we shared, never
Will be forgotten, reflected forever.

To Tiko

The purring presence has passed away,
    She won't be with me to greet the day.
I loved her so well
It's impossible to tell
What she went through
    The ups, the downs, the pain, the joys—
She watched me and played with her toys.
Goodbye, my best friend!

Matiko

loving, determined,
purring, rolling, playing,
always in my heart,
CAT!

Ode to Tiko

Alone, but never quite alone —
There is your empty chair,
Yet sometimes in the shadows
I imagine you are there.
My companion , all your 18 years,
No longer here with me —
Still in some very special way
You keep me company.

Morning Reverie

Chirping birds lift their joyful song
    To the dawn,
My heart can but sing along
    Like a fawn.
The sun, the moon, the stars rejoice
Soul, mind and spirit add their voice.

To greet another sunny day
Helping me go down life's way
My purring cat on my lap
Ever gently reminding me that
This is God's world; He's in control —
A soothing balm for my soul.

Two Purrfect Pets

Matiko and Sweetie
Both the embodiment
Of God's love on earth,
Both loving, playful,
Happy cats —
    With strong personalities,
    Strong attachments,
    Strange voices.

Two close companions
    Sharing my life, my bed,
    My joys, my sorrows,
    My travels and trials,
      My quiet times,
      My work and friends.
    Making an apartment,
A hotel room, or even
    Mother's home — a haven.

Purrs, pets, playful touches
    Adoring looks,
    Contentment in tucked-in paws,
    Happily blinking eyes.
    Rubs and happy rolls
Welcoming me home
From a 12-hour day
Or a trip downstairs.

Someone to care for
To meet her needs,
    To hold her and talk to her.
    Somehow a part of
    The same universal
Spirit and consciousness —
    Matiko and Sweetie.

Spiritual

JEANINE ALLISON

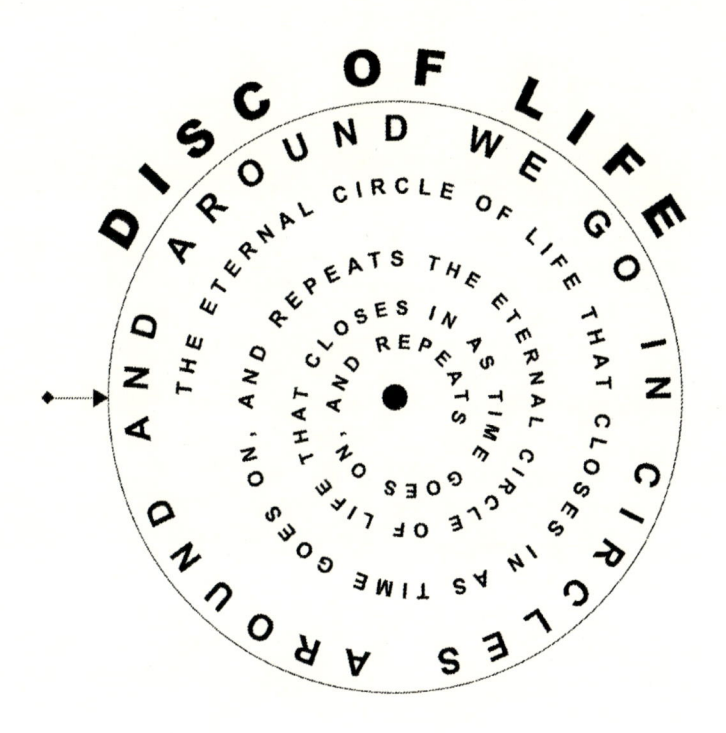

DISC OF LIFE

AND AROUND WE GO IN CIRCLES AROUND AND AROUND

THE ETERNAL CIRCLE OF LIFE THAT CLOSES IN AS TIME GOES ON, AND REPEATS THE ETERNAL CIRCLE OF LIFE THAT CLOSES IN AS TIME GOES ON, AND REPEATS

Whispers in the Wind

Blossoms in Spring

The soft pink petals
Form a carpet on the ground,
And I tread gently
Listening to the faint rustle
As my feet shuffle through
The tree's discarded beauty;
Blossoms whose youth
Is past and makes way
For the fruit to grow
And ripen, offering in
Maturity nourishment
For man's body,
As the scent and
Color and shape of
The blossoms in spring
Did for his soul.

Time's Healing hands

Again I turn to Time's healing hands,
Not uncertain of how it all stands;

"Wait and see," it's difficult and yet
Time has taught me that's the best bet.

Action and changes, my customary stance,
But perhaps it's not Time for the big chance.

The hurt, anger, sorrow will diminish, I know,
And Time will reveal what it has to show.

*The Occult**

Strange powers, magical bonds,
Unexplained meetings, certain rounds,
Shifting fortunes, unusual ties,
Uncertain outcomes, "necessary lies."

Strong affinities, powerful "pulls,"
Numerous coincidences, sudden lulls,
Unleashed storms, peaceful pauses,
Workable potions, unknown causes.

*The Occult—"beyond human understanding, mysterious"—from Websters' New World Dictionary, 3rd College Edition

The Future

Magic, cards, astrology—all those
Attempts to ask One who knows.

The secret of the Future locked, you see,
In the past of all of us, even me.

We want to foresee, to be prepared
To take advantage of good times shared.

We want also to know about the bad
To heed a warning so as not to be had.

Seekers, all of us in a foreign land,
Anxious to learn what we have to stand.

A Dream...a Warning

My life is the bus
That is racing downhill
Its driver frozen in fear
The electrical system
Not operating —
No brakes!

Faster and faster
Toward a huge truck
In its path.
I close my eyes
So as not to see
The inevitable impact,
Praying but unafraid.

The Shadow of Your Wings

I am safe, enfolded in the shadow of Your wings,
I can relax and rest assured, so my heart sings;
My every trouble, toil and care
    You find a way my grief to share.
    You rest my soul, my burden make light;
    You help me daily to do what's right.
And as I go to You in prayer
    Your wings of love make everything fair.

The Waiting Game

To live in Greece
Is to learn to live
With uncertainty.
Θα δουμε*
Wait and see.

For problems here
Have a way
Of resolving themselves,
If patience
And prayers
Can help us
To let the threads
Of time
Unravel themselves.

Waiting, however,
Means we hand
The reigns
Of power
To someone else
And to trust
That those hands
And the final
Outcome are
Guided by
A stronger
And surer
Force.

Θα ζουμε!**

   * Θα δουμε — We will see.
 ** Θα ζουμε! — We will live.

Home Safe Harbor

My home, my sanctuary, my refuge, my
    joy—
A place to retreat for rest and relaxation,
A source of renewal in rigorous reflection,
A place of silence or neighborhood noises.
The music of the radio keeping me
    company
With Tiko curled contented on my lap,
My plants waiting to be watered,
Books to read, marking to do
Letter to write, God's abundant supply
Of food and refreshment, clothes to wear
To fix, to change, accomplishment in
    presenting
An image to the world
My phone and computer, my link,
My safety, my communication.
A prayer of praise and thanksgiving
For what God has offered and
My guardian angel protects.

Easter Renewal

Summer time
As the clock moves forward
    The lilacs bloom anew
    Resplendent once again
    In royal purple
    Turning up happy faces
    To catch the dewdrops
    Deliciously sparkling
    In the gentleness
    Of early morning sunlight.

The God-given rain
    Soaks the waiting earth
And the promise of spring
    Of joy, rebirth, revival
Once more fulfilled.

A Little Prayer

Thank you for the flowers
    that grow
Peeking shyly through
    the snow.

Thank you for the
    evening breeze
Wafting gently through
    the trees.

Thank you for my
    nightly rest
As ever, You know
    best.

Where I need to
    rest my head
You provide a
    welcoming bed.

Thank you for the
    morning light
Shining softly, after
    the night.

"Thank you for the birds
    that sing
Thank you, God, for
    everything."

Whispers in the Wind

Reflections

Whispers in the Wind

What If?

Sifting through the sands
of memories,
elusive,
only a touch, brief, a little
painful
not sharp—a dull ache,
of things
that might have been—
but maybe
we wouldn't have
wanted them
if they had...
existed.

La soledad de muchos años –
Una vida bastante larga
Experiencias de muchos cosas
Muy diferentes de las de
Otras personas,
Muy distintas.
Memorias felices o tristes
Todas mias!
Ahora puedo olvidar
Si no quiero pensar
En los amores de
Mi juventud, o puedo
Recordar con una
Sonrisa, de alegria
O de tristeza.

JEANINE ALLISON

(English Translation)

Misty Memories

The nostalgic feelings of many years
A life, long enough
Experiences of many things
Very different from those of
Other people,
Distinct, indeed!
Memories, happy or sad –
All mine!
Now I *can* forget
If I don't want to think
Of the loves of
My youth, or I can
Remember with a
Smile, of happiness
Or of sadness.

Promises

Too many heartaches, promises broken
Too much pain for hasty words spoken
The circle of regret, unfallen tears
The bitterness that dulls only with years.

Enjoy the elusive happiness highs
Revel in the ecstasy and sighs;
For everything we get we must pay;
We all do, whatever we may say!

Think carefully, then, before saying "Sure."
The injury done can be without cure.

Peek

Most of the time
I keep my feelings
Tucked away securely
Deep in my pocket.
Sometimes they want
To peek out again
To test the waters
Of reality. Is it
As harsh as always?
Well, yes, it is —
And so, they scurry
Back to a safe harbor.

Ripples on the Pond

The undisturbed peace of the pond
Invites us to throw
A small pebble—and see
      what happens.

Dare to cast that pebble
To disturb the silky serenity
Of the pond's surface.

Watch the widening ripples—
The circles of involvement,
Tiny waves of exploration.

Pick up another pebble,
Toss in a different direction,
Observe the resulting ripples

Ripples radiating out
      from each splash
Actions and reactions
Ever-widening circles
      on the pond.

Cause and effect, a chain
      of events
One action the catalyst
For another and another.

Dewdrops

Dewdrops glistening on
    blades of grass
Glimmer in the early
    morning sunlight,
Sparkling like rhinestones
    reflecting joy
Of a new day to be savored
Before the burning heat
    makes these gems
Disappear into the air
Of the workaday world,
To be lost in the
    menial minutae
Of obligation, observations
    and opportunities
Each day encompasses,
Until the welcoming twilight
Slows down the merry-go-round
Of daily life, promising rest
For the weary,
And overnight
the humidity forms into
    tomorrow's dewdrops.

Time

Time is my friend
 but he's also my enemy.
  He helps me get over
   the emotional pangs.
  He chases me on
   busy days.
    As he is devoured,
     he devours my plans
     and my hopes.
      He rushes by me
       like a free, fast-
        flowing river.
         He stops and picks
          me up and
           carries me along—
            until that
             magical day
              when I can
               be in perfect
                harmony,
                 with
                  him.

A Tarot Reading

The world turns—
The wheel of fortune
Is upside down,
Again!
But the final outcome
Is the Sun
And it is
Right side up,
This time.
The lovers along the way
—the "beginning of a
possible romance."
Ah well,
As the Spanish say,
Todo es posible
en este mundo*.
Possible, but is it
Even desirable?
And if I had it,
Would I want it?
Life's a game of
      cards,
And it is hard to win
In straight poker.
The Tarot answers,
      "Maybe."

---

* Everything is possible in this world.

Reflections on a Rainy Night

I felt at last I'd
Met someone
Who wasn't like the
Rest.
But once again I've
Been deceived —
You couldn't stand
My test.

Perhaps I expect
Too much,
But someday I will
Find
Someone who can
Surely measure up
And calm my
Restless mind.

Surfing

Empires are built
And fall.
The tide goes out
And returns
To shore.
Fortunes are made
And lost.
Life is a series
Of waves,
And we are on a crest
And fall
To the depths
Once again—
But able
To rise once more.
We must be
Like expert
Surf riders—
Try to ride
The crest as long
As possible.
To feel the high,
The power,
The peak!
The thrill of
Being on top!

But then a slip,
The wind shifts
Abruptly, and
Our board
Goes our from
Under us.

We hang suspended
A moment
And then
The *crash!*

But still
"The goin' up
Is worth
The comin' down."

Yes, Kris*.

* With a nod to Kris Kristofferson,
his songs, beliefs and life.

Search for Myself

Who am I?
Where am I going?
When will I be settled down?
Why do I travel?
What is the purpose of the trip?
Whose path am I following?
What will it be like?
What sort of result can I expect?
Which idea inspired me?

Questions without answers!

But the quest goes on
Until we reach the end
And ask ourselves
The final question,
Was it all worth it?

First Day Confusion

Noise, unexpected and
Anticipated changes;
Disregard of plans
And feelings,
Lack of caring,
Sharing our misery.

But, in the midst,
A smile —
A flash of understanding,
Joint laughter.
"It doesn't matter;
We'll get by."

The first day of classes
Sorts itself out
And we've lived
Through it again.

Phantoms

Images drift across
The years, covering
The gaps of time and space
Between what I was
And what I am.
But it's all shrouded
In an elusive shifting mist
That too easily masks
The truth, along with
The hurt, and
Softens the edges
To blur the outlines
And the boundaries
Between fact and fantasy —
What was and what
Might have been —
Floating and fragile,
Change, reform,
Drifting and dreaming;
The future caught
In the net of the past.

JEANINE ALLISON

*Arachne**

Caught in a trap—
Of my own making,
Having become
Too dependent
On the bonds
Of money.

It ties me, too,
And pulls me toward
A way of life
I thought
I had left behind.

Illusions—the power
Can too easily
Ensnare even me,
Who knows too
Well the
Implications
Of the inescapable
Silken web.

* Arechne is a Greek myth about a girl who was turned into a spider by the Greek Goddess Athena for challenging the goddess to a weaving contest.

At a Crossroads

I sit and wonder,
"Which way?"
I, who always
Have alternatives!
Seldom am I
Bewildered
As to which to
Take.
If I go one way —
Unhappiness.
If I go another —
Regret. (Oh hell!)
Another still —
Temptation
(Am I weak?)
And the last is
Disaster.
And so I say,
"Which way?"

Choices, Dreams and Circles

Reality and illusions—
A dream world of refuge
Where things work out—
But, of course, they don't!
You don't believe in
Happy ever after,
But maybe you'd like to.
You know too well
What "sweet dreams" are;
And they're not
Any different today.
The theme remains
The same, though
The characters and setting
May change and
We may rework
The plot.
The wheel of fortune
Spins or turns slowly,
But 'up' today
Is 'down' tomorrow.
And Fate reaches out
To take a hand
Again, standing back
Smiling—waiting
To watch the effects
Of a light touch
Or a decisive push.

Life Isn't Fair!

We live with whatever Fate deals
Not knowing what our neighbor feels.

Saying to ourselves, "I will survive,"
In the end, of course, we won't be alive.

The struggle, the pain, the sorrow, the trial,
The unfairness, exploitation against
      which we rile.

But we can't change the firing,
The deportation; the end is tiring.

Paradoxes and Circles of Life

    We live close together
    And we stay far apart.
    We never know if another
    Speaks from the heart.
    Time rushes on, but
    The memories stay.
    Another game won,
    A marvelous day!
    Then another game lost,
    The circle slowly turns,
    We're faced with the cost—
    The bitterness *burns*...
    Paradoxes and circles of life.

My World

In the world of wealth
The values are different;
Manipulation, cheating,
A bargain ill-won—
These are what
It's all about.

It's not my world;
I don't sell out;
I won't touch
Their tainted money.

I belong to the workers,
And I can't feel
An affinity for
Another group
As here, I belong.

Everything I have
I've earned
—in spades!—
But I wouldn't
Accept it
And really
Wouldn't want it
Any other way.

Webs

The webs of life —
The cobwebs in the corner,
Things left unused, undisturbed.
The sticky webs
Meant to catch
The unsuspecting
Who venture
Too close —
Caught!

Too many tied to
Various things;
Bonds of silk
And love;
But they're
Not free.

I'm free —
No webs in my life!
But did I pay
Too high a price
To cut
The silken ties?

I Am What I Am!

I'm free because I refuse all ties;
I'm honest and turn away from lies,
I'm warm and caring to my friends,
But *not* to those who use me for their ends.

I'm helpful and loyal, gentle and true,
But my true traits are known by few.
I'm strong and happy with a ready smile,
Someone to count on during a trial.

But I'll do exactly so much, and no more—
Not that I'm afraid of any chore;
I refuse to be used and cast aside
Left to be washed away with the tide.

I'm approachable and respond to those
Who appeal to me, regardless of clothes;
I'm friendly to those who deserve my trust,
But beware of saying to me, "You must!"

Life is a game, and I'm a good player
Never just another "Yes" sayer;
I know that I stand for and who I am
From now until they tell me, "Scram!"

Determination

To find myself
I had to learn
What I was *not!*

What I didn't
Really want
And wouldn't accept.

No compromises
For me,
I am what I am.

And I'll stay
Being that
For always.

Face It!

Another crisis, a serious one.
A contract not renewed —
But known really for
More than a year.
An abrupt change
In attitude, perhaps
In life style, once again.

But, if I left a husband,
A country, a secure job
Voluntarily and came
To a foreign land
With little money
And fewer possessions,
Not knowing the language
Ignorant of the customs
With nothing certain
Ahead of me —

I can do it again!

Free

I want to break free
Free from the ties
Of a job, even a country
And a home I love.

My life still goes on…
Got to make it on my own!

Hidden Mirror

Dreams and paradoxes
Is nothing what it seems?
Do we all wear masks
To hide from ourselves,
Even in the mirror of life?
And if our real selves
Were to peek through
For an instant
Would we even
Recognize them?
Or like my cat,
Would we draw back
From the stranger
In the mirror?

Around

Circles. Spirals, webs,
The wheel of fortune,
Images of life
Going around
The circle game.
But there's no
Escape.
We can move
But only within
The set ruts.

Illusions of progress
Looking at the world
From a different
Perspective.
But nothing really
Has changed.

Under Capricorn

The mountain goat
A solitary creature
Independent, proud,
A survivor —
Needing little!
Surveying the
Green valley
Below
But aloof
From it and
Other mundane
Matters.
Climbing toward
The peak
Pausing to
Raise his head
Showing his
Determination
To be what he
Is.

In the Candle Glow

The softness of the candlelight
Shimmers in the warm velvet night
Imparting to it an afterglow
Hiding what it oughtn't show —
The lines of hurt, tear-bathed eyes
Legacies of too many futile tries.

The years are blurred; candles flatter —
Not that it should really matter.
But sometimes it still does, you see,
Even to someone as determined as me.
A hesitant smile, an implied invitation
Ready for another uncertain situation.

The Game

I lost a hand
But still managed
To win the game.
Now I can break
The poker face
And still sit back
With a smile
To bask in the comfort
Of knowing
That the winnings
Belong to the survivors.
In the end
I held the ace in the hole —
Competence.
High card —
And game!

The World Turns

In the world where
Favors are bought
And sold,
I stood a little
Apart.
But in the end,
Will I too
Be willing
To pay the price
For a little
Security?

The Surface of Life

I used to deplore
Those who lived
On the surface of life —
But no more.
Perhaps I have now
Only a nodding acquaintance
With myself.
The real *self*
Is hiding —
Hurt too many times
To venture out again.
Not afraid
But wary.
Taking my pleasure
Where I find it,
Leaving a smile,
A nod — occasional
Nostalgia,
Not caring to 'care.'

Ebb Tide

The chances I missed,
the connections we
    *almost m*ade,
but the waves
roll in
and the tide
    pulls back
and the patterns
    on the sand
disappear.

And when they
form again
it's never the same.

Something is lost
    never to be
    regained.

The spiral, not
the closed circle.

Nostalgia

My mind drifts back, over the years
The hopes, the ups, the downs, the fears
The smiles and frowns, kisses and sighs
The feeling one can make it, if she tries.

We want to return to a simpler time
When we were assured and in our prime
Through the mist of memory to the past
To the joys, sharing, caring that didn't last.

Every coin has its opposite side, you see
Everything "held" wants to be free.
Live for today, dare to be bold,
Don't feel you've been left out in the cold.

The pendulum swings, fortune's wheel turns
The future reaps what someone earns.
Remember always but don't feel sad
And don't try to regain what you never had.

Christmas Cards

Capturing memories
Messages of shared
Emotions, experiences, excitement…
Joys and sorrows
Of the roller coaster of life.

Communications across the years,
Across the miles.
Cementing lasting friendships,
Even of friends not met
Face to face
For many years.

What we were; what we have
Become; what we hope for
The future — uncertain at best
Sealed in a card
With the usual wishes
And greetings of the season
Sent with affectionate
Closings — a handclasp, a
Kiss in an envelope.

IF

Sifting through the sands
of memories,
elusive,
only a touch, brief,
a little painful,
not sharp—a dull ache
of things
that might have been—
but maybe
we wouldn't have
wanted them
if they had...
existed.

A Song for Friendship

Loving, caring, helping friends
Celebrate the joys of life together,
Smooth out the bumpy roads of life,
Walk with us when we feel alone,
Share toils, trials and tribulations,
Pop the cork and savor the sweetness
Of the champagne of blessings showered
Down, through God's great grace.
A guardian angel folds protective wings;
The cat purrs contentment,
And our universe unfolds, as it should.

Letters

Messages of love and caring
News and views
Ideas and Ideals,
Photos and features,
Keeping in touch
Across the miles
With many old friends.
Poetry and prayers
For relatives and friends —
Sharing the minutae
Of our lives; thoughts
And details dovetail
In daily touching base.
Making connections,
Caught in a common
Web of affection —
A kiss and a caress
Sealed and sent
In an envelope, by post.

Masquerade

We wear our masks to school each day,
We take our places, on stage, in the play.

Our moves are planned, our speeches set
The performance goes on, whatever we get.

The roles we play may vary a bit,
And we're never sure they'll be a hit.

The director may demand something new
We're never sure what we have to do.

The masks cover up what we really feel
Dances effectively choreographed, *not* real.

The setting, the props, the costumes, our
    roles;
The play's the thing — but it takes its toll.

The teachers' masquerade, the music starts —
Does it reflect what we feel in our hearts?

Fragments of Joy

A dozen women on a lazy Saturday
Afternoon, writing in community,
Removed from the Athens bustle,
Birds singing without the
Background drone of traffic,
Palm leaves swaying gently
    in the breeze
Cats and dogs as cozy companions—
    Friendships,
    Roses
        And
        Gentleness,
        Meaningful
        Elements
        Needing
        To
        Share.

Fragments of joy in the little things,
Kindness, consideration,
A glimpse of eternity.

Rainbow of Life

Red signals danger
Stop and wait—
Orange is both
Excitement and caution,
Yellow for happiness
Joy of the sun,
Green symbolizes
Nature and youth
Blue means rest
Relaxation and comfort;
Indigo is the mystery
The enigmas of life;
Violet it the one
That represents me!

After the Play

How lonely the theater is!
The sets have disappeared—
The boards we trod are
Worn and needing paint.
The backdrop is gone,
The set of drums sit
In isolation on the
Stage, the seats so recently
Full of enraptured spectators
Are empty and looking a bit
Threadbare in the harsh
Light of reality. The royal red
Carpet needs vacuuming;
There's talcum powder the
Actors used to tone down
The shine of faces damp
With the reflection of the
Burning footlights and
Individual spots. The
Backstage area is cleared;
The whispers of anxious actors,
Dressers, and curtain pullers
Only an echo in the shadows
Of the dream world, of the
Make-believe that we
Were able to impart to our
Audience, and transport them
With us on journeys to other
Times and places, exotic and
Mundane, joyful and grieving—
The end is the beginning
In another hand in the
Circle game of life.

Solid

What is solid in my life?
Sweetie says, "Me!"
My love and devotion
Sincere and strong
The power and determination
To stay the course
Solid achievement
Rock solid friendships.

The Key

The key lies before me —
Tempting, golden, precious;
I have only to have the
Courage to reach out, to
Make it mine.

Like Macbeth's dagger,
I wonder if it's real!
The three acorns like the
Three witches, expressing
Hidden thoughts.

It can unlock my fetters,
Set me free from drudgery
Too many hours,
Too little return!
Dare I grasp it?
Turn the lock?

Cobwebs and Cables

Habits hold us in their hands
Willing us to go down the old familiar
Well-worn path, even if we want
To try that road less traveled.

Each time we repeat those habits
The ruts in the regular road get deeper,
The cable that connects us to the past
Grows stronger, reinforced with
    ribbons of repetition.

Meanwhile, the sunshine sparkles
On the cobwebs crisscrossing the
    unused path
Way down ahead, on the gossamer
    threads
Waiting for a courageous wayfarer

To venture through the shadows
Down that shady, seldom-trod
Narrow, winding, inviting trail
To tomorrow's dreamland, and
Brush aside the cobwebs, to see
    the hidden rainbow.

I Hear Greece Rejoicing
(In deference to Walt Whitman's "I Hear America Singing")

I hear Greece rejoicing —
    the diverse loudness I hear:
The crash of plates on a marble floor
    defiantly breaking in triumph,
The clapping of upraised hands,
    the snapping of eager fingers
In time to the mournful yet
    happy rhythms of the bouzouki,*
The twisting and turning of energetic
    dancers in native costume,
The harmonious enjoining of voices,
    singing of challenges met
Hardships overcome
    difficulties faced down,
The celebration of an indomitable spirit —
The shouts of *opa***, *ela**** to
    demonstrate the *kefi*,****
The thud of jumping feet
    landing in a victory dance,
The swish of shoes in a circle dance
    on the cement patio
        outside a village *taverna*,
Young and old,
    wizened grandfathers,
        and gurgling babies,
Toddlers squealing with delight,
    grandmothers cackling with joy,
Voices raised together in the unquenchable
    celebration of life lived to the full.

*   Greek stringed instrument
**   Ola — Exclamation of joy or a sudden happy feeling
*** Ela — *Come on!*
**** Kefi — In a good mood to succeed

Afterword

Whispers in the Wind

Thoughts and Questions

The setting was in the quiet countryside of Vrilissia, welcomed by a massive, friendly, golden-beige dog guarding Kiki's wonderful sanctuary. Late afternoon, early spring sunlight streamed in the westward facing window, joy light to write by. Two soft silky tri-colored cats visited the writers, adding their purrs to the hum of voices and then 20 women settled back into the lengthening shadows, to pour their thoughts and feelings through their prose onto the paper. Sensing security swirling around them, a suitable place to commune with one's muse.

One cat contentedly curled up in a director's chair and went to sleep, the ultimate companionable cat – Mrs. Simpson.

Time stretched out before us like a highway in the desert. Enforced time for rest and relaxation that I suspect we seldom make, but should!

And what will we discover as we travel down that highway? What surprising circumstances lie in wait around the next corner? Unsure of our destination, should we stop or continue? We're not sure if we should go on, or decide we've reached our destination and stop and rest for the night.

How seldom we have two uninterrupted hours to sit and think, to delve deeply into ourselves and write – whether journal writing or letter writing. It's *time* for a change. I'm afraid to claim it, but I need more time, TO BE, more quality time to just BE ME!

The dust will still be there. Sweetie has her biscuits. Turn off the bells of the phone and just disappear inside. Do I dare?

The scene shifts to another setting – Martha's Vineyard, humid summer heat, a safe country-like environment, women writing in community there, too. Some friends of many years in both places and some unfamiliar faces drift in and out of consciousness, sharp edges blurred by the softening of time. Always cats – another memory of my beloved Tiko, gone now for almost a year, but Sweetie has come to take her place – both females too, part of the special feminine mystique that joins us like "the silken ties of love and thought." My personal narrative that summer, in the nervous nineties, was "Sometimes we have to be transplanted in order to bloom." And I wrote back then about how I blossomed in Greece.

Something intangible holds me here still and provides the fertile soil to keep replacing the withered leaves that fall from the stem with delicate new green leaves like the promise of early spring. The cycle of life continues; the wheel turns.

What if it were Sweetie there – would she be able to accept confinement to a bedroom, hearing the many voices outside? Maybe she could more easily live in the kennel. And what will I do with her as I go on tour and travel for exams? Maybe it would be easier for her to stay with someone. But what about me? Can I face the trials alone?

"What else do we share but being women?" is a good question. We share the affinity for delving into feelings, the love of animals, the nurturing instinct, the openness to share, the willingness to be part of a community and the acceptance of being quiet. I can't imagine men doing this. It has to do with sensitivity, but Whitman or Williams would be happy here.

"Writing to learn" as valid now as in another summer workshop where we kept our moon journals. We need to come apart and rest a while in order not to come apart in fact. We need to stop and take stock of who we are NOW, and where we're going. Are we on the right road or did we take a wrong turn somewhere? Should we backtrack and find the right road again? Was it when as Frost says, "Two roads diverged in a yellow wood," or was it at a far less obvious junction?

Do we have to keep on traveling? Why have I gone back to two different positions that both involve extensive traveling and both involve education? If I was going to look for new dimensions in life, in middle age, why these exactly? I say it's for the money, but is it really? Am I avoiding other obligations?

Besides the two cats and two new jobs, what other twos are currently significant in my life?

If I could "look into the seeds of time" and see which will flourish and which will not, would I really do anything very differently?

I enjoy experiencing a lovely big home, but I really think I wouldn't want one. I prefer the coziness to open spaces to live in. I don't think it's sour grapes/sweet lemons, but maybe it is.

How much communication is now based on e-mail! Does it bring us close together or is it *really* socially isolating?

No longer do I go out very much. At times I'm busy, and/or tired, but at others I really *could* go. Why don't I?

Rhetorical questions – questions without answers – but good to think about.

About the Author

Jeanine Allison once wrote in one of her many journals, "Some people have to be transplanted in order to bloom." Like Ulysses, Jeanine has been seeking her *Ithaca* for more than 20 years, and in the sometimes turbulent sea of life, writing journals and poetry has been her anchor throughout her explorations of both her inner and outer reality. Through these journeys, she has completed undergraduate degrees in English and psychology at Queen's University in Kingston, Ontario, Canada, and history at the University of Toronto, also in Canada, as well as a masters degrees in statistics and overseas administration at the University of Toronto and the College of New Jersey in the United States respectively. Post-graduate U.S. writing courses from Northeastern University and the University of California together with acting and singing have enhanced other responses to her creative muse.

Printed in the United States
4705